ENDORSEMENTS

Equal parts charming and deeply reflective, Michelle Seitzer's THE
DICTIONARY OF GRANDPARENTS takes you on a journey to remember the humans who made you who you are today. She expertly weaves
together delightful stories, beautiful poetry, and thoughtful prompts
into an invaluable exploration of capturing what matters most. In a
world that's increasingly fleeting, Seitzer's book reminds us of the power and richness of reminiscence.

> – **Melody Wilding, LMSW**, author of *Trust Yourself: Stop
> Overthinking and Channel Your Emotions for Success at Work*

We sometimes forget our beloved elders had lives well before we showed
up on the scene. They had hopes, dreams, and experiences that colored
both their childhood and the families they created as adults. In THE
DICTIONARY OF GRANDPARENTS, Michelle Seitzer brings them to
life on the page through a vivid array of stories, prose, and poetry, while
providing the reader with an inspirational blueprint for doing the same.

This heartfelt look into the history of those who influenced who she
is today feels like the antidote to a digital age that constantly bombards
us with shiny, new, and fleeting. What she has created is the gift of a
lifetime by opening her eyes and her heart to the past. She has offered
us the same.

> – **Judith Henry**, author of
> *The Dutiful Daughter's Guide to Caregiving*

The Dictionary of Grandparents

An Alphabetical Guide to Mining Your Memories

MICHELLE SEITZER

Revelation 1:19, The Holy Bible, Modern English Version. Copyright © 2014 by Military Bible Association. Published and distributed by Charisma House.

Quote from "Now and Forever," by Ray Bradbury: ©2007 Ray Bradbury (P)2008 Recorded Books, LLC

All dictionary definitions: © 2023 Merriam-Webster, Incorporated. All rights reserved.

Cover & interior design by Typewriter Creative Co.

ISBN 979-8-9878924-0-4 (Paperback)
ISBN 979-8-9878924-1-1 (eBook)

DEDICATION

Dedicated to Alice & Peder Pedersen and
Donna & Warren Snyder, and to all the other sets
of honorary grandparents I've collected along the way.

TABLE OF CONTENTS

FOREWORD

"Write the things which you have seen,
and the things which are,
and the things which will take place after this."

- REVELATION 1:19[1]

"No sound, once made, is ever truly lost.
In electric clouds, all are safely trapped,
and with a touch, if we find them,
we can recapture those echoes of sad, forgotten wars,
long summers, and sweet autumns."

- RAY BRADBURY, *NOW AND FOREVER*[2]

INTRODUCTION

This is a collection of poems and stories about some of the most precious people in my life, my grandparents.

I want to pause here and say that if you didn't have a good relationship with your grandparents, or if your grandparents died before you were born, lived far away, or weren't the kindest of people, please keep reading.

This book is still for you, because I'm certain there's at least one person in your life – a great aunt or uncle, a family friend, a long-time neighbor – who's been a stand-in, honorary grandparent. So from this point forward, if the word grandparents brings up complicated or unpleasant feelings and memories, refer to that dear person in your mind who is or was like a grandparent to you.

I created this book to showcase all the ways my grandparents' influence – and genetics! – shaped me, and to emphasize the importance and value of reminiscing about them, all within the framework of 26 words (one for each letter of the alphabet).

Each chapter contains a poem and a short story/essay that gives context to the designated word, and ends with a question to guide your reminiscing or imagining. You may use the prompts to sketch a memory, jot down a story, take notes from a discussion at family dinner, or simply to reflect on the warm memories of the "grands" in your life.

How I arranged this book

Here are the components from which this book is built (all definitions are from *The Unabridged Dictionary by Merriam-Webster,* unless otherwise noted):

Dictionary
"a reference book listing terms or names important to a particular subject or activity along with discussion of their meanings and applications"

Grandparents
"a parent's parent; a grandmother or grandfather"

Reminiscence
"a remembered experience"

Imaginings
"products of the imagination"[3]

About the imaginings: There's a technique some writers use in creative non-fiction called "perhapsing"[4], and it's a bit like artistic license in a movie, where details may be filled in with imaginative embellishment or speculation because the hard facts are not available or cannot be verified by the person in reference. This can be for any number of reasons: the person is no longer living, the person has a memory or communication impairment, or the details are foggy in that person's mind (which can happen to any of us!). Memory is a finicky and mysterious thing.

I'm fascinated by this technique, and in the pages of this book, I used it to close some gaps in character sketches or stories – as my grandparents are no longer here to answer questions or tell me stories I didn't know about. While I verified some things with relatives, I wanted this book to be about my own reminiscences and imaginings, from my perspective and memories.

My grandparents all had very distinct accents related to their home and heritage: Brooklyn-Italian, and Norwegian. You'll see a lot of Norwegian words throughout this book, and hear/see their unique dialects on the page too.

Why we must remember (even the things we don't know yet)

Statistics say the average person lives within the space of three generations. After you die, you are most likely to be forgotten after three
generations, on average.

And yet: stories surpass these statistics. Stories secure your place
in the memory banks of your descendants, they affirm your ancestry,
and they connect you to parts of your past you may never know unless
these stories are shared and passed on.

Like the caverns of the cenotes, your family history is waiting below
the surface – deeper and wider than you can imagine – and your
grandparents are the gatekeepers. If you have them here, tap into that
inkwell. If you only have a picture, use it to imagine who they were
and are, and how they've made you.

Your family's stories can go on for generations, backwards and
forwards. But it's up to you to preserve the ones that matter most,
to mine your memories, and to care for the spun threads of your life
story and legacy.

That doesn't mean everyone should write a book or that you have
to record your family's entire history from the beginning of time, for
all time. What you can do is curate a collection of favorites, of the
things that should never be forgotten, of the moments you'd like to
replay and access even if your memory should fail you. And you can
start right now.

ANCESTORS

*"one from whom a person is descended and who is usually
more remote in the line of descent than a grandparent"*

WALTER AND AGNES

ANTHONY AND LUCY

WILHELM AND JENNIA

THORVALD AND AMANDA

These are my ancestors, my great grandparents, the parents of the people I had the honor of calling grandparents. Even though I never met them in person, I'm always connected to them by genes, stories, documents, and photographs. My ancestors gave me life; their blood runs through my veins.

Before you meet my grandparents – the stars in this particular galaxy of stories – allow me to introduce their parents: In portraits knit from tiny threads of stories other people shared, colored by the people they carried to birth, and who are now carried to the page by my own imaginings.

WALTER <u>AND</u> AGNES
- PARENTS OF GRANDPA WARREN -

Great Grandpa Walter

When I imagine Walter, I think of the parts of my father that are parts of me: an unassuming timidity allied with an unswerving loyalty that's both endearing and enigmatic.

A height not only impressive in feet and inches but also in the measure of a deep soul.

A softness and a roughness that was only there because it had to be – but when you got to see the softness unbridled, you never felt anything so comforting, so free, so secure.

A craftsman humble and skilled whose knowledge is profound and purposeful, he tinkers until he gets it right and then tinkers some more, simply for the joy of the process.

Great Grandma Agnes

When I imagine Agnes, I think of elegance and pragmatism, the quintessence of woman, wife, giver, and distinctively independent individual.

She's wrapped in a dark blue-gray pea coat with a bright floral silk scarf that's blowing in the brisk wind she's bundled up against.

She is the resilient part of me that persists even when the rocky cliff she's standing on is crumbling, sending off scatterings of gravel and chunks of stone into the sea below.

She tightens her vibrant scarf around her face, tucks in her curls, and lets the ocean wind redden her cheeks.

ANTHONY AND LUCY

- PARENTS OF GRANDMA DONNA -

Great Grandpa Anthony

When I imagine Anthony, I breathe in the music of the Italian coast and picture overflowing plates of pasta, stemless glasses of wine, and cold dripping pitchers of water placed on a long table – wrapped around by friends and family who only stay in their seats long enough to eat and spend the rest of their time dancing.

He's bold and brash and buoyant because he's loved and loves back. He doesn't skimp on the relationships that matter and he is generous with boundaries when the protection of what is precious requires it – no matter how small the amount or immeasurable the treasure.

He bounces the littlest ones on his knees and invites the oldest to hold hands and spin around the Maypole, ribbons unfurling and flowers in the girls' braids that are flying behind them.

Great Grandma Lucy

When I imagine Lucy, she forms the scents and sense of all things made by our family from then until now and forevermore, the seasoning that's proprietary, personal, and peculiar.

She's wearing an apron deftly tied and dotted with thousands of yellow and orange flowers that you can't tell are flowers – unless you look closely and brush away the flour.

She is patiently and vigorously stirring a brown enameled pot and it's brimming with something that's rich and nourishing, refreshing and simple, complex and delicate.

She's a force that's not forceful and a reckoning that walks the line between modesty and extravagance, a line no one dares to cross but everyone wants to get a hair's breadth away from, to sit in the white-hot tension, enamored by its ardor, held in her glow.

WILHELM AND JENNIA
- PARENTS OF GRANDPA PEDER -

Great Grandpa Wilhelm

When I imagine Wilhelm, I picture a desk he loved to sit at when the farm tasks were done for the day. He'd pick up a pencil and paper and put his hands to a different kind of work, one that relied more on his brain and less on the muscle memory "to do" list he'd been completing since the sun came up.

On the page, he was free to speak up and shout out in a way he couldn't imagine doing in real life; on the page, he could push the limits of the everyday box he found himself in.

He didn't mind that everyday box, but those fleeting moments when his mind was completely untethered, his rough-hewn pencil gliding across the smooth, crisp paper – these were the moments he lived for.

Great Grandma Jennia

When I imagine Jennia, I wonder how she decided to become a *jordmor* (midwife), and whether she anticipated staying overnight in people's homes, supporting the laboring mother around the clock, carrying a pressed white nightgown in her leather supply bag just in case.

When she got back to her own home after a long shift of bringing a baby into the world, I imagine she would try to sleep, but her thoughts were like nurse's shoes squeaking up and down the lengths of hospital linoleum, running in and out of rooms to check on the newly born children and their bewildered or exhausted parents.

I think of how she never really stopped working, because the care and keeping of her own large family was always waiting for her, no matter how hard the labor and delivery of the day before.

She is the part of me that is bound to her loved ones with an indefatigable dedication, and her sacrifices often go unnoticed – even to herself – until she finds herself in a place of utter exhaustion from the ceaseless caregiving.

THORVALD AND AMANDA

- PARENTS OF GRANDMA ALICE -

Great Grandpa Thorvald

When I imagine Thorvald, I see a quiet soul living in the nebulous space between fully content and hopelessly restless, a cup of *te* (tea) always at hand, and a half-finished book beside it.

Outside his bedroom window a bird is building a nest and he finds himself relentlessly drawn to that spot, observing the mother's painstaking process of stick gathering and intricate construction. The tiny bird does her work methodically, creating a densely packed home with a flotsam of found objects to keep her young safe and comforted.

He isn't flustered when others mock his love of feathered friends, and it's not shyness that keeps him from playing with peers. There's just too much to read, and books are his truest companions. (And he wears his heart on his sleeve only when he imagines himself as the hero of his story.)

Great Grandma Amanda

When I imagine Amanda, I think of soft hair the color of coffee that's heavy with cream, and rosy, round cheeks that look like the two high arches of a hand-drawn heart.

A collection of farm animals large and small are following her lead as she heads outside for another chance to bury her face in her horse's mane and nuzzle her cheek against his strong neck.

It's nearly noon and she completes her morning chores on her own time, dawdling and driven, a free spirit who practices compliance for her parents' sake. She closes her eyes, draws in the full aromas of her horse's thick mane, and pictures herself riding, trotting, galloping – both of them leaving the farm to roam the full expanse of the countryside she calls home.

She goes back inside to start preparing the *middag* (midday) meal, her gaze always wandering to the window and staring out at the land whisper-shouting her name.

This poem was inspired by a photograph recently discovered on Ancestry. com. It was taken on my great-great grandparents' 70th wedding anniversary.

Those hands!

I just saw a picture of my great great grandfather
I'd never seen before.

It was my dad.

My dad's pensive upside down smile,
the kind he makes when he's deep in thought –
and not because he's mad or sad.
Lips pursed, teeth hidden,
his mouth mirrors the shape
of his arched eyebrows.

His eyes are intense:
focused,
dark,
somber –
like he's pondering
the weight of the world
or waiting for someone
to tell a joke
or just doing as he's told:
"Sit still, don't move."

The outline of his face, chin, and neck,
his ears,
his hairline –
marked by fine, spiky, salt and pepper hair,
residing at the back of his head:
All a perfect match.

His hands are exact replicas,
in shape,
position,
mass,
and measure.

It's astonishing how much their hands are alike.

He is wearing a tie,
a black vest,
a white dress shirt –
and I can see
his shoulders
have the same slope
and thinness
as my father's.

I just saw a picture of my great great grandfather.
I just saw a picture of my father.

RECORD, REMEMBER, REFLECT

From memory or imagination (or a combination of the two), create a portrait of a great grandparent that represents characteristics of you and your family.

_____

_____

_____

_____

_____

_____

_____

_____

_____

_____

_____

_____

_____

_____

_____

_____

BELOVED

"dearly loved : dear to the heart"

From my first breath, my first thoughts, my first words – my beloved grandparents were my favorite subject.

They continue to be the embodiment of feelings that strike way, way down in my being, like a neatly woven network of nerves, scents, sounds, and visuals.

They are the definition of history, heritage, and legacy – all wrapped up in a bundle of delightful and soothing memories. As I've revisited these memories, I've learned this truth: I measure so much of my life in the time before and after grandparents.

And now, it's time for you to meet them. Allow me to introduce the main characters of this book, the subjects of all my heart-written words in the pages to follow:

WARREN AND DONNA

my father's parents, of varied European and Italian descent

PEDER AND ALICE

my mother's parents, of Norwegian descent

WARREN <u>AND</u> DONNA

Grandpa Warren

My paternal grandfather died before I was born. I never held his hand, but he is part of my body. I didn't get to know him, but I love him. He seemed to live in a silence that was brooding. But not necessarily in the dark way of the word. Rather, it was like he wore a wool blanket cape to shield him from the bumps and bruises of life.

Grandma Donna

My paternal grandmother loved out loud and lived that way too. She wasn't shy about her feelings in any way, and I admire that about her now more than I had the capacity to in my younger years. She never did anything half way unless that's how it was meant to be done – and even then, she was all in. The things I never want to forget about her are her boisterous voice, bubbling laughter, and wholly expressive face.

Warren & Donna were the proud grandparents of 8 granddaughters and one grandson. Many great grandchildren would follow.

PEDER <u>and</u> ALICE

Grandpa Peder

My maternal grandfather smiled with his eyes and loved people with every happy-tear-filled glance. He was a craftsman through and through: an expert carpenter and woodcarver, a technician and an artist. He was strength and humility personified. He was joy and kindness wrapped up in a tall, handsome, gentle, loving, and lovely man. There was no one like him.

Grandma Alice

My maternal grandmother had a grace and beauty I've yet to encounter again. She looked like a movie star – as a young woman and as she bloomed into her 90s. Glamorous and gorgeous but so very shy and quiet. Stylish and neat, precise and pondering everything, she was stronger than she appeared and had a depth – and a mischievous side – that wasn't readily visible. And at the edges of her, a sadness she kept close to her chest.

Peder & Alice were the proud grandparents of 8 granddaughters and one grandson. Many great grandchildren would follow.

This poem is about the sound and sensations that align with the spoken word, "beloved."

The Love We All Want

A word reserved for only the dearest:
beloved.

Simply say the word,
b e - l o v - e d
And I promise you'll feel
a heart-squeezing fullness
a full body sigh
a smile at the corner of your lips and your eyes

It's like there's a hug right there in the word
Be lov ed

Be loved.
Beloved.

To be loved by someone,
to be someone's beloved,
to call someone your beloved.

This is the love that lasts a lifetime.

And this is the deepest of human hopes:
To have this kind of beloved love for any amount of time.

It is a gift to be beloved, and to have a beloved (maybe even more than one).
That is the love we all want.

RECORD, REMEMBER, REFLECT

What do/did you love most about your grandparents? How would you describe them to someone?

COMFORT

*"contented enjoyment in physical or mental well-being
especially in freedom from want, anxiety, pain, or trouble"*

Grandpa Peder had the most amazing hands.

In the church he helped build, he designed and fabricated a 15-foot-tall wooden cross which still hangs in the sanctuary today, the place where we sang one of his favorite hymns, "The Old Rugged Cross," at his memorial service. And one year for Christmas, his hands made jewelry boxes for all eight of his granddaughters in a stunning *rosemaling* (traditional Norwegian wood carving) design.

He had the kind of hands that didn't hesitate when cutting down and chopping up a fallen tree to use the wood for his projects, the kind of hands that didn't flinch when guiding that found piece of pine, walnut, or cherry through his table saw (even though I would flinch from the shrill sound of wood hitting blade).

When he was happy to see his grandchildren and hear their latest news, he'd clap his big hands together in absolute delight and smile his broad smile.

When he met someone for the first time or was greeting an old friend in church, he'd shake their hands firmly but with such warmth and exuberance you felt like royalty.

When the neighborhood kids rode their bikes past his house, he'd come down the driveway and put his hand out for a "low-five." After they slapped it, he'd pull his hand away quickly, shaking it as if it had been burned by the intensity of their slap. Then he'd wink so they knew he wasn't really hurt. Little did they know how tough and strong this man's hands were – and how much pain those hands had experienced...

Though he hated talking about it, Grandpa was a prisoner of war when the Germans occupied Norway during World War II. He was taken to the northernmost part of Norway, hundreds of miles and many fjords and mountains away from his home in the southernmost coastal region.

His woodworking apprenticeship interrupted, his new job in the work camp was to use those skilled hands to build tunnels through the snow, tunnels through which the Germans would pass their weapons. As he told me, they were given little to almost nothing to eat, so he and the other prisoners would often dig through the snow to find food.

When he told me this story years ago, he looked at his hands. He had also looked away to hide the tears collecting in his deep set blue eyes. They weren't twinkling as they usually did. I didn't ask any more questions.

Those strong and sinewy, scarred but soft hands held the babies he helped his midwife mother deliver. Those hands held his own three children, countless nieces and nephews and great nieces and nephews, nine grandchildren, and the two great-grandchildren he lived long enough to meet. He cradled their tiny heads in those powerful hands.

Over the eight-plus decades of his life, his hands probably spent the most time clasped in prayer. His faith was the foundation of his life, the core of who he was.

In his final months, bedridden by Alzheimer's, we held his hands in ours, praying he'd feel the comfort we wanted to deliver, the strength we wished we still felt in his hands. He experienced hallucinations as part of his dementia, and sometimes we'd see him raise his hands, motioning with his fingers at something on the walls.

We couldn't see what he saw, and it was devastating to see his fear and confusion and not be able to clear it. But then sometimes, we'd feel him squeeze our hands, and it was a fleeting but tremendous gift.

I can't manipulate a piece of wood with my hands the way Grandpa could. But when I'm creating a new piece of writing (which he was always proud to read), greeting someone new, or holding my daughter's hand for comfort or safety, I hope I'm carrying on his legacy of craftsmanship, care, and compassion.

And maybe that's why years ago, when a dear friend complimented me on the character of my hands, the words went straight to my heart.

This poem is all about the foods, items, places, and people from which we derive comfort.

Comfort Comes in Many Forms

> A plate of pasta
> A cup of tea
> A bott-uhl of bee-uh*
>
> *Comfort comes in many forms.*
>
> A downy pillow
> A woodstove's warming glow
> A blanket knit by loving hands
>
> *Comfort comes in many forms.*
>
> A quiet tune, hummed low and slow
> A gentle tap-tap-tap, whispered on your palm
> A word given, with hope inside
>
> *Comfort comes in many forms.*
>
> A beloved grandparent's steadying hug
> A beloved grandparent's reassuring smile
> A beloved grandparent's knowing glance

Comfort comes in many forms.

The right portion
The right measure
The right cadence

The right dose of ease – at the right time – to soothe
whatever ails:

Comfort comes in many forms.

*a bottle of beer, spoken in Grandma Donna's Brooklyn-Italian accent

RECORD, REMEMBER, REFLECT

What distinctive feature or quality of a grandparent delivered a sense of comfort?

DESCENDANTS

"a lineal or collateral blood relative usually of a later generation"

In the upstairs room of a refinished barn overlooking the North Sea, there was a gorgeous old piano, cast iron farm tools hanging on the wood walls, and several long tables to seat dozens for a family reunion I attended in Norway, held in 2017.

We gathered in the warm evening light to have a meal together, and as the guests arrived, they stopped first at a table set in the front of the room, topped with sepia-toned photographs of our ancestors, whom we all shared but had different names for – *mor, bestefar, tante, søskenbarn* (mother, grandfather, aunt, cousin), depending on our relationship to them.

About midway through the evening, after the meal, everyone turned their chairs forward and the dining room became a concert hall.

The adult children of Great Grandma Jennia and Great Grandpa Wilhelm stood at the front of the room and told stories, shared memories, explained connections.

Then a young cousin came forward to play another rousing tune on his *hardingfele* (Hardanger fiddle), and I surveyed the room from my corner seat. My eyes landed on my daughter, who was holding hands with the relatives on either side of her, her arms swinging and lifting theirs, their feet stomping in time on the plank wood floors.

My heart swelled up with joy and grief.

Over the course of the celebration I'd been studying the faces in that room, awestruck by the show of genetics. I saw a girl who was a carbon copy of a cousin back home. I saw a ten-year-old and a thirty-year-old who had our great grandfather's distinctive ears. I saw my mother talking to a cousin who could have been her twin sister.

And then, my daughter. Deep, dark eyes, caramel-toned skin, brown hair as dark and rich as the way Norwegians take their coffee.

She certainly wasn't the only person there not of the family bloodline; there were in-laws and many children of all ages who were the blend of their parents (myself included).

But then I wondered: will she ever get to be in a room with her people? Will she ever get to see what ancestor she resembles, or meet a cousin who could be her twin? Will she ever get to gather around a fire playing instruments and dancing until dawn with her family (which is how I imagine it would happen)?

The answer is unknown. Unlikely, but not impossible. I will hold on to hope that she'll have a family reunion experience like this.

And yet, there she was – in the middle of the action, in the middle of so much love in the room, in the middle of a string of people who had linked their arms together with hers to dance – and she belonged there. She was welcome there. She was grafted, grandfathered, and grandmothered in by love – in a way that surpassed biology, blood, and genes.

She is my descendant and I am part of her tribe, and though her biological family tree may be dotted with question marks, there's absolute certainty in the ties of love that bind her to ours.

As I wrote this book, I was struck for the first time with this thought: I might not become a grandparent in a biological way. This poem was inspired by that realization.

Descendants

Who will my great grandson be?
Will I have a great granddaughter that looks like me?
I have not given birth to a child.
I have a child that may not give birth to a child.
I have a child who does not have my genes or DNA.

Will I have a granddaughter?
Will I have a grandson?

I may not.

And if I do,
she, he, they
will not look like me.

There are many ways to pass down love.

There are many ways to leave legacies in places and people unrelated to you by blood or marriage.

My descendants don't have to look like me.

My descendants will be the people I love who come after me.

RECORD, REMEMBER, REFLECT

Have you ever attended a family reunion and saw yourself in someone there, or found a twin in an old photograph?

_____

_____

_____

_____

_____

_____

_____

_____

_____

_____

_____

_____

_____

_____

_____

ECHOES

"the sound due to such reflection"

When I went to Norway in 2017, I unexpectedly met a man who was delivered by my great-grandmother, Jennia, the *jordmor* (midwife).

It was about halfway through our two-week trip and I wanted to see the cemetery where several of my relatives were buried, particularly, Grandpa Peder's parents. I had seen where Grandma Alice's parents were buried when we visited in 2010. I wanted to complete the circle, to stand in front of their dates and names and connect with them that way.

Norwegians are very deliberate and thoughtful when it comes to visiting the deceased. They do it regularly, respectfully, and with great care – a ritual that is not morbid but deeply meaningful and often involves caring for the earth around the tombstone. The surviving visitor usually comes with garden tools in hand.

I discovered this on our last trip after nearly every family member we visited – even one as young as 13 – took us to a cemetery to meet someone whom we could no longer meet in the flesh.

So now, on a cold, misty July day that felt very much like a dream, my cousin and I approached *Vanse Kirke* (Vanse Church) in our raincoats. As I took in the size and scope of the cemetery, I wondered if I'd be able to find them – because it was much bigger than I expected – and the relative accompanying me was from the other side of the family.

I was only discouraged for a moment, because we soon saw a man who appeared to be a caretaker at the church, working in the yard. We approached him, and my cousin explained in Norwegian who we were and why we were there. He answered in English, and looked over at me as he said, "Jennia Pedersen? She delivered me. Follow me, I'll take you to her."

My heart exploded. Was this really happening? Did I really just meet a total stranger in a Norwegian church cemetery in 2017 who knew where to find my great grandmother, born in 1893 and died in 1972, the woman whose hands, skill, and vocation were part of the reason he was standing in front of me?

The echoes from below the earth were loud that day; the reverberations from this circular connection like the rounded ripples of a stone breaking the mirror still surface of a lake. Not only did I get to see my great grandparent's names and dates on their stones, I felt their presence through this caretaker.

I thought of Great Grandpa Wilhelm, who stayed home with the kids when his wife was called to work the unpredictable shifts of home labor and delivery. I thought of how my Grandpa Peder would sometimes accompany her on house calls. A family business in every sense of the word, built on caregiving and skill and compassion and erratic hours. And in that reflection, I see myself.

A few years ago, I decided to take my daughter with me to the cemetery where Grandpa and Grandma are buried. I worried it might be too much for her emotionally, but I knew she had been missing Great Grandma, and that she's very in tune with people who have gone before. Now, she comes with me every time we stop by.

(((*echoes*)))

If you shout loudly enough, you'll hear them.
If you listen closely enough, you'll feel them.
Electric, they are.
Hidden from sight, but not from sound or reverberation.

Bouncing, chasing, tunneling, running,
Pulsing, playing, hiding, coursing.
Circuitry, it is.
Circles closing in on themselves and rippling outward.

Clouds gather above my grandparents' gravestones,
My knees dig in to the squishy earth,
flattening the cool green grass and marking my skin
with the imprints of each dewy blade

The clouds are shaped like two people holding hands
The sun slices through
My daughter says she hears great grandma talking to her
Our eyes well up

We leave before it starts raining.

RECORD, REMEMBER, REFLECT

Where do you see parallels with your ancestors and family reflected in your own life?

_____

_____

_____

_____

_____

_____

_____

_____

_____

_____

_____

_____

_____

_____

_____

_____

_____

FORTITUDE

"strength of mind that enables a person to encounter danger or bear pain or adversity with courage"

My sister once called Grandpa Warren "the stranger" when she saw a picture of Grandma Donna next to a handsome but unrecognizable man in a Navy uniform. Grandma always laughed at this classification of her husband, who died unexpectedly at age 52 and therefore never met any of his grandchildren – aside from seeing a hospital photo of the oldest one, and hearing her crying over the phone.

What I've learned about Grandpa Warren is that the air and sea were a big part of his life and work. He attended the New York School of Aviation Trades, a vocational high school, and when World War II started, he joined the Navy, where he was assigned to an aircraft carrier and performed maintenance on their planes.

It was a carrier escort, a smaller ship which served as security for the larger ones and for the battleships in the convoy. Grandpa Warren's ship number was CVE94 (Carrier Vessel Escort), but the crew would joke about this title, saying it stood for Combustible, Vulnerable, and Expendable due to their smaller size, slower speed, and significantly less armor plating.

Their job as tenders of the CVE was to protect the bigger ships at all costs – human and otherwise. In the Pacific where they served, the small-but-mighty CVE94 saw quite a bit of battle action, sustained minor damage at the hands of a Kamikaze war plane, and was once caught in a major storm that tossed the carrier escorts around like toys.

A book was written about these brave ship-tenders and appropriately titled *The Little Giants.*

As I think about these experiences of "the stranger" who is the father of my own father, it's hard to picture him as anything but strong, brave, capable, determined. He was all of those things, in my mind. He'd have to be to survive such an assignment, and yet it's hard to reconcile these truths with the other handful of things I know about him, things I've only been told in passing.

The story of his death is a heartbreaking one: he collapsed suddenly on the subway platform on his way to work – a cardiac event – and my father, also on his way to work, found him there.

Fortitude is forged not only in moments requiring courage on stormy, war-tossed seas. Fortitude is forged in moments of facing actual death – expected and unexpected, your own or someone else's – and not also collapsing yourself. Fortitude is forged in moments of darkness so black that all light is swallowed inside it, and not a single speck gets out.

Fortitude runs in my blood: the blood of "the stranger" and his son and me.

This poem was inspired by my delightfully tough as nails Grandma Donna and her Brooklyn brownstone, which felt a lot like a fortress in size and structure.

Fortitude

> The stoop was as hard
> As the sidewalk it led to
> The one she pushed her rolling cart down
> To fill up with groceries
> Intensely independent
> Robustly self-reliant
>
> My Grandma from Brooklyn

RECORD, REMEMBER, REFLECT

What's the hardest thing your grandparents ever had to face in their lifetimes? Did it break them or build them up?

GIFT

CHAPTER 7

"something that is voluntarily transferred by one person to another without compensation: the act, right, or power of giving or bestowing"

I could never leave a visit with Grandma Alice without something being shoved into my hand.

And I'm not exaggerating when I say shoved, because Grandma Alice's enthusiasm always showed up in her hands.

She was a quiet woman of few words. Her face wasn't as expressive as Grandma Donna's, but that didn't mean she was unhappy or emotionless. Stoicism and introversion are among the hallmarks of Norwegian culture, and she modeled both well.

And when it came to her family, there was no holding back, no reticence or restraint or regulation – she'd pat you on the back with the full force of her love.

This was a reminder that you were loved and you were hers.

But she also took great delight in transferring something from her hands to yours – quite often, a $20 bill rolled like some tiny paper cigarette or folded like fabric origami.

It happened the same way every time. After an hour or two of visiting together, she'd walk me to the back door (only guests and delivery personnel used the front door – a rule that stands to this day, because Grandma Alice and Grandpa Peder's house stayed in our family).

We'd stand in the small hallway that separated the main area of the kitchen from the back door.

We'd say our goodbyes, hug, and then she'd grab my hand and push the gift into it, closing her hand tightly around mine so I couldn't drop it or try to give it back.

After many years of politely refusing or resisting these exchanges, I finally realized that by doing so, I was taking away her joy in giving.

And so I began receiving these hand-to-hand communications with an open heart, knowing the real gift wasn't the money but the transaction – the bestowal – of her love into my palms.

This poem needs no explanation.

priceless

No gift-wrapped present from my grandparents
will ever match the gift of their presence.
Grandparents are the gift of a lifetime.

RECORD, REMEMBER, REFLECT

What's the most memorable gift a grandparent gave you?

_____

_____

_____

_____

_____

_____

_____

_____

_____

_____

_____

_____

_____

_____

_____

_____

_____

_____

HANDIWORK

CHAPTER 8

*"work done by the hands: work done personally: personal
or individual achievement"*

I love that all of my grandparents worked with their hands. Grandpa
Peder built houses and carved wooden treasures with his hands.
Grandma Alice made endless meals, desserts, hats, scarves, and blankets with her hands. Grandpa Warren used his hands to hold tools
for examining and inspecting aircraft. Grandma Donna used a typewriter in her administrative job and was a genius with her hands in
the kitchen.

My grandmothers' handwriting in birthday cards and recipes will
always be like mini pieces of artwork to me.

Grandma Alice always signed cards with exclamation points: "Love
from Grand-Mom & Grand-Pop!" (even though that's not what we
called them) – so I know where my enthusiasm for that type of excitable punctuation comes from.

Grandma Donna's handwritten recipes are my favorite ones to use,
because it's like she's cooking or baking beside me when I look at her
careful, controlled script.

When I think of my grandparents, I often think of their hands and
all the care they delivered, all the things (edible and otherwise) those
hands produced, all the times each one sat at a desk to use those
extensions of themselves – to write a card to a precious grandchild, to

send a donation to a cause they believed in, or to write down a recipe for future generations to recreate. Those hands reached into the future that way.

This poem is about Grandma Alice's love of knitting and crocheting. I have so many memories of her sitting quietly by the pool or on the couch, watching her grandkids play, her hands busy.

love is handmade

Knitting needles
Crochet hooks
And busy hands
Produced without patterns
Colorful afghans with open panes
We loved to poke our fingers through
Soft scarves and warm hats
With decorative emblems
To adorn her grandchildren's
Necks and heads
And at night, the tools were
Tucked away neatly
In a wooden framed
Dusty rose fabric
Hammock
Next to the couch
Ready for her next
Handmade piece of
Handiwork.

RECORD, REMEMBER, REFLECT

What kind of things did your grandparents make with their hands? What kind of work did they do – from household chores to professional jobs – and was it hands-on?

INSTRUMENT

CHAPTER 9

"an implement used to produce music especially as distinguished from the human voice"

Nearly every time my daughter plays her harmonica, I think of Grandpa Peder, who was a terrific harmonica player. I think of his hands shimmying up and down the instrument, his eyes either closed in concentration, or looking at us for our smiles and applause, his cheeks pulling in and out with each breath. His youngest brother also loved the harmonica, and I remember the two of them playing hymns together when he and his family were visiting from Florida. It was heaven on earth.

I was thrilled to learn my Great Grandpa Anthony played numerous instruments too – guitar, violin, banjo, mandolin, clarinet, and: harmonica. According to family recollections, when the extended family got together, he would break out his guitar with a harmonica attached and play the old standards while everyone sang. This was decades before I was born, but I can picture the scene in my mind, can picture my daughter dancing in the middle of the room as she does now whenever and wherever music is played.

Music is a magical glue that binds memories, generations, people from different countries and decades of history, and family – even family who aren't bound by DNA.

This poem was inspired by an afternoon spent exploring the contents of Great Grandmother Jennia's midwife bag.

Handheld

When I got to hold in my hands
the medical instruments
my great grandma once used
to bring babies safely into the world,
It was like we were holding hands
with just a few decades between us.

RECORD, REMEMBER, REFLECT

What objects do you still have that belonged to your grandparents or ancestors?

JUNK

"something devoid of meaning or significance"

There's no story I wanted to hear more than whichever one my grandparents wanted to share. But there were some stories they weren't fond of sharing, stories they never volunteered.

And for Grandpa Peder, those stories were from his experience as a prisoner of war during World War II (which I referred to in chapter three).

It started with an assignment for a high school history class, the standard "interview someone who lived through the war" type fare. I jumped on the opportunity to get some stories out of Grandpa, who hated talking about himself in any way, shape, or form.

Nevertheless, I knew he wouldn't refuse his insatiably curious writer-granddaughter. For privacy and focus, we conducted the interview outside on the porch, sitting face to face in plastic chairs with nothing in between us. Me with my pencil and paper on my lap, him with his hands folded in his.

It was like pulling teeth to get him to talk.

I could see that the subject matter – and the sharing of it – troubled him deeply.

It pained me to see him that way. So I didn't push or probe too much, even though I wanted to learn as much as I could about his extraordinary bravery in unfathomable circumstances.

But the thing that pierced my soul the most was what he said about these stories.

"You don't wanna hear about all dat yunk," he said, indicating my furiously scribbling hands then looking away, as if he hoped a different, brighter story about that dark, dark period of his life would materialize.

"Grandpa! This stuff is not junk. This is your story," I said, pleading with him to recognize the incomparable value of his personal narrative – as far away from junk as ever a thing could be.

I wrapped up the interview, knowing the little he shared was precious enough. Besides, his comfort was more important to me than getting all the details – especially if doing so meant bringing traumatic memories to the surface.

I understand now how complicated talking about trauma can be, no matter who the audience is. In fact, I think there are cases where the more beloved the person (the listener), the less you want to share the painful parts of your life with them. It's a form of protection.

And I'm fairly certain this is why Grandpa Peder didn't share more. Yes, he was modest to a fault. Yes, he didn't believe his story was worth my writing a school paper about – it was "yust yunk," as he said.

But above all, I believe he didn't want his granddaughter to know how harsh the world could be, how harrowing life was during those days that must have felt like years, how hopeless he must have felt despite being naturally optimistic.

Stories are best remembered when they're shared. But how do you know when the pursuit of a story results in too much pain? How do you know when to push forward for the sheer value of those hard-won stories, and when to squeeze the brakes?

Read the room, the person and your relationship – and check your motivation. You'll find your answers there.

This poem is a reminder to slow down, especially in moments of grief.

precious things

When your grandparents die
Don't be quick to throw out their junk
In case you find
Something springs to mind
An object of theirs
Precious only to you
Junk is in the eye
And heart
Of the beholder

RECORD, REMEMBER, REFLECT

Was it hard to get your grandparents to tell you their life stories or did they share openly? What are the things you were most surprised to learn?

KINDRED

"a group of related individuals: one having community of interest or close affinity with another"

When you grow up on a dairy farm in a country whose inhabitants live as close to the land as their own skin, skim milk is an absolutely unacceptable option for afternoon *kaffe og kake* (coffee and cake). Or really, for consumption at any time of the day.

Grandpa Peder always reinforced this truth, calling it "dat awful gray stuff," and saying the words with such disdain that an argument would be absurd.

Milk should be pure white, thick, rich, crisp, creamy, wholesome, nourishing, sustaining – all the things that skim milk most certainly is not.

The watered down version of milk had no place in Grandpa Peder's fridge unless one of his beloveds needed it. And so it was grandfathered in, residing on the shelf beside the container of whole milk, looking like the impostor it was.

He would never drink it himself. Nor would he tell his grandchildren not to if that was the drink they really wanted. But he by no means would support its existence, praise its value, or affirm it as milk.

This declaratory firmness softened by the deepest of love is what made Grandpa Peder the bedrock of our family, the solid foundation upon which our memories were built, the compass you'd never lose your way with.

You knew where you stood with him, always. Anyone who knew him felt this way: from the waitress he just met to the neighbor kids from down the street who never filled his mailbox with shaving cream like they did the others.

He made you feel like you were the only person in the room and someone worth taking great delight in, and he showed that delight in his crinkly smiling shiny blue eyes, and the way he'd clasp your hands in his or shake your hand with such earnest enthusiasm you didn't know whether to laugh or cry.

But as a grandchild, your footing was secure in a special way. You knew where you stood: as close to him as his own skin. And no skim milk substitute would ever do.

Being embraced by him in a sturdy, standing hug – the one where my ear was pressed to his beating heart – that's the place I miss the most. In that place, nothing else mattered. In that place, the boom of love was deafening.

When we were preparing for our first trip to Norway in July 2010, a year and a half after Grandpa's final homegoing, I ached for that proximal place and knew that I'd get close when we were there.

The proxy was one of Grandpa's brothers, one he was close to in age and friendship, and one we all knew quite well because he'd visit the United States often.

My great uncle was built differently; he walked with a rocking sway in his hips and had a lightness about him in structure and substance. But he was tall like Grandpa Peder and had smiling eyes too, though his were a lighter shade of blue and his twinkle one of mischief and fun.

Early on he taught us girls a little Norwegian, as in – how to ask Grandpa for money (*kan jeg få noen penger?*). We laughed every time he said it.

When I got to Norway that summer, I knew a standing hug from him would be the closest thing to hugging Grandpa I'd get on this side of heaven. As Grandpa's kin and my own. Pressing my ear to his heart, his arms encircling, as close to me as skin in the land they both were born in.

From this vantage point over a decade later, I can tell you the moment of that hug was just as wholesome and nourishing and rich as I yearned for it to be. It wasn't Grandpa Peder. But it was an acceptable and worthy substitute, one I delighted in, and? One that also made me miss him more.

This poem is about the complicated nuances and simple love between the people we call our "family."

Kindred

> We're not cousins,
> But our moms are.
>
> She is not my flesh and blood,
> But she's my daughter.
>
> When all three grandparents were together,
> All was right in the world.
>
> Your tribe,
> Your kindred,
> Your people
> Are wherever
> And in whomever
> your heart rests secure.

RECORD, REMEMBER, REFLECT

What/who makes you miss your grandparents the most?

LORE

*"something that is learned: a body of traditions relating to
a person, institution, or place"*

Grandma Donna was always up for a good story, and I remember her
telling one that involved lupini beans, an apron, and dirty fingernails.
The thing is, I can't recall now whether it was an ancestor who sold
those beans straight from her apron, or if it was just Italian folklore
told with the dramatic flair that imbued every Grandma Donna
story. All I remember are those three concrete details and how hard I
laughed at Grandma's masterclass in storytelling.

Family lore is a precious gift, and if you are blessed enough to
know some of yours, I recommend writing it down or even recording
yourself talking about it. Because no matter how unforgettable those
characters and tales seem, your memory is often an unreliable narra-
tor who is guilty of picking up brain bits and bobs and making connections where there are none, convincing you that the moving parts
of a film scene actually happened in real life.

But when you look at the definition of lore, there's more to it than
stories – it's lessons, it's wisdom, it's a transmutation of belief. Maybe
it doesn't really matter who the lady selling the lupini beans was, or
whether she was a distant relative or a completely fictitious figment
of Grandma Donna's imagination. Maybe what's passed down to the
generations after me is the art of the oral story, Grandma Donna style,

and the lesson being: "Don't tell a story unless it's a good one; embellish if you must."

When Grandma Alice was in the twilight of her lifetime, before her cognition was altered by strokes, I remember feeling like I'd run out of things to talk to her about. This made calls somewhat painful in that they were drawn out, full of silence and repetition, and almost always ended with guilt-laden turns of phrase like "When are you coming home again?" or "No one ever calls me." I never wanted to feel like a call to Grandma Alice was a chore I didn't have time or energy for – nor did I ever want her to feel like she wasn't worth a ring.

So I consulted my first love, stories, and made a plan to ask Grandma to tell me a story or two from her life – whether it came from her childhood in the hills of Norway, her marriage to Grandpa Peder, or her job in New York City. Whatever it was, I wanted to hear it. Whenever I'd call from that point on, after we'd done the standard greetings and questions, I'd ask her to tell me a story.

I didn't keep up with this new tradition as consistently as I'd hoped, but I enjoyed hearing these new and as yet undiscovered stories about her on a regular basis. There were two that stood out in my mind: one that involved a brother putting his hand down a pig's throat to grab a treasured, gifted watch, and the other involved Grandma Alice and a brother in a small row boat in the middle of a lake, swallowed by the fear of never getting back to dry land.

Family lore is full of meaning. Stories like these are never mere memories or fanciful facts. They are legends and lessons and left-behind bread crumbs along a family's terrestrial trek.

I wish I had asked for more stories from both grandmothers.

I wish I had written them down.

I wish they were still here to tell me more of them.

But I will persist in passing them on. I will persist in pushing others to do the same.

Tell your family's stories. Learn your family's lore. Give future generations the gift of knowing the history, heritage, heroics, and heart that makes your family unique – the shield and crest that protects and preserves, and holds your place in the world.

This poem is a push to preserve.

Red Ribbon Words

Write the stories you must remember.
Write who you should never forget.

Write what they said when you forgot to listen.
Write what you want to remember when you can't.

RECORD, REMEMBER, REFLECT

What are some of the most memorable stories and tales in your family's history?

_____

_____

_____

_____

_____

_____

_____

_____

_____

_____

_____

_____

_____

_____

_____

_____

_____

MODESTY

"freedom from excess or exaggeration : moderation: free-dom from conceit or vanity : an awareness of one's limita-tions: limitation in size, amount, or extent"

My grandparents were all very modest. Even Grandma Donna in her boldness had a sense of modesty about her.

But something that all three grandparents were not shy about? Their unconditional, unbridled love of their grandchildren.

They were exceedingly generous and unabashedly proud of their family – their children, grandchildren, and great grandchildren.

They bragged openly about our accomplishments and never missed a birthday party, school play, band concert, wedding, college tour (Grandma Alice and Grandpa Peder took me to see Eastern University, my alma mater), or any other important life event to which they were invited and included.

Something I'll always treasure is the way Grandma Donna couldn't stop talking about my performance in a third grade play. I don't re-member the name of the play, but all the characters were sheep, and I was the bookish, nerdy one named "Woolhemina."

The whole weekend she was at our house for that performance, she would walk around saying, "My little Woolhemina," and squeeze my cheek with so much force I had no choice but to smile. Even weeks and years later, she'd mention it with glee. She loved the theater, and loved to boast about any of her grandchildren who pursued it, keeping playbills and stage photos in a special frame.

That kind of pride and preservation is so valuable to a growing child, and so meaningful to the adoring adult on the other side. We should never stop celebrating the things that are worth preserving, and we should never dim our adoration for the accomplishments – no matter how seemingly insignificant – of those we love.

This poem is about the way modesty runs in my family, on both sides.

Modesty, juxtaposed

I hold up the shy modesty of my Scandinavian heritage
(Vikings, in sheep's clothing)
Against the hardy audacity of my Italianness

And the contrast amuses me, delights me,
makes sense to me
and of me.

But even my Italian ancestors and relatives carried a sense
of modesty.
Yes, even the ones who were
forward in their love
and forward in their living
had modes of operation mired in modesty.

The most modest of the Norwegians
had audacious ways of living and loving too.

And so: I've turned the word around in my mind accordingly.

RECORD, REMEMBER, REFLECT

What did/do your grandparents like to brag about? What quality or characteristic dominates one or both sides of your family?

NOURISH

*"to promote or stimulate the growth or development of :
to provide with sustenance: to furnish or sustain with food
or nutriment: to cherish or keep alive (as a feeling or plan)"*

When I think of all the things I ate at my grandparents' homes over
the years, I am grateful for such loving nourishment:

...like a simple summer snack by the pool made special by Grandma
Alice's presentation and service,

...or a robust Italian meal at Grandma Donna's where every inch of
the table was covered with food, including bowls of fusilli noodles that
were as curly as my hair,

...like a warming bowl of soup, pasta *"fuhzool"* (pasta fagioli) made
by Grandma Donna or *ertesuppe* (split pea soup) with ham made by
Grandma Alice,

...or a breakfast of "tin pancakes," which was Grandma Alice's way
of saying "thin pancakes," or *panekake*, which are essentially the
Norwegian form of crepes.

All were made with so much love and comfort infused, it's no wonder so many of my happiest memories with my grandparents involve
gathering around a table.

I also have wonderful memories of going out to eat with my
grandparents.

One of Grandma Donna's favorite restaurants in Brooklyn was

Junior's, home of the famous New York-style cheesecakes. One year, we all went there to celebrate her birthday. Her vivacious joy was the most memorable part of that meal.

Grandma Alice and Grandpa Peder would often take me out to dinner when they'd come to visit me at college. Grandpa would order his favorite – spare ribs – and I loved watching him interact with the server. He'd say things like "How ya doin' there young fellow?" or he'd give the waitress a compliment that made her smile.

Other favorite family food outings included Sunday brunch after church, Chinese food feasts around Grandma and Grandpa's kitchen table, and trips for Italian ice (chocolate was the best flavor, of course) and pizza from Gino's in Brooklyn.

Baking in the kitchen with both grandmothers sticks in my mind as a treasured reminiscence. Both Grandma Donna and Grandma Alice made marvelous desserts: Italian seven layer rainbow cookies with apricot jam; Linzer cookies dusted with powdered sugar and a chewy raspberry center; Norwegian waffles with butter; crispy, delicate *krumkake* (a waffle cookie shaped like a cone); and *risgrøt* (rice pudding) or *riskrem*, served warm or cold with cinnamon or fresh strawberries.

Food multiplies in value when it's made by – and shared – with the ones you love.

This poem speaks to the life-giving relationship that is grandparenting.

grandparent communion

There's nothing as good for the mind, soul, and body
As good grandparents.
Be one now.
Become one now.
Shared blood and relations are not requirements.
Nourish yourself by nourishing another.
Grandparents are all around,
And we never outgrow our need for them.

RECORD, REMEMBER, REFLECT

Talk about all the culinary favorites in your family. What were some of the most memorable meals or traditional celebrations involving food and grandparents?

_____

_____

_____

_____

_____

_____

_____

_____

_____

_____

_____

_____

_____

_____

_____

_____

ORDINARY

CHAPTER 15

*"regular, customary, or ordinary condition or course of
things : such as is ordinarily met with or experienced"*

Having such magnificent grandparents as a grounding part of my life
was anything but ordinary, but it was a steadfastness that I relied on, a
steadying undertone that couldn't be shaken. Until it was.

It was just an ordinary day while living in Baltimore in the early
2000s when Grandma Donna came to mind. Just as quickly I thought,
"I'll call her tomorrow, she'll be around."

And then she wasn't.

I didn't know I should have called.

She wasn't ill.

She was as healthy and independent as she could be, just like she
always was. And so I thought, "I can call her another day." But then,
I couldn't.

Grandpa Peder had been in the grip of dementia for eight long
months, confined to his bed, but there were no recognizable signs that
the end was near. His death, relayed over the phone, was also unexpected. I didn't get to say goodbye, and that was devastating.

Grandma Alice lingered for weeks after a stroke, which wasn't her
first – but the damage sustained from the others made this one something she couldn't bounce back from, no matter how resilient she was.

I was determined to be there for her final minutes.

I was not.

She was alone: none of us were there for those final minutes, but we had all been able to say goodbye in our own way.

In those long weeks, I got to spend many, many sacred and mysterious and poignant and powerful moments by her bedside. Holding her hand. Touching her hair. Sitting at her feet. Waiting, waiting, waiting. Wondering when, and how, would it happen – and would I be there in that moment of transition?

As I said, I was not. Perhaps she wanted it that way?

Death is a highly personal thing. There's nothing ordinary about it, and yet, it happens every single minute of every single day. And it will happen to all of us.

The grief I experienced when I lost each grandparent was extraordinary, because that's what the love we had was: extraordinary.

I miss every ordinary moment with them, and wish they were here for more. But – I'll take extraordinary love over ordinary love any day.

This poem is about the moment I found out Grandpa Peder had passed away. I went home and sobbed loudly for most of the day – and for many days after.

Where were you when...

On just an ordinary day,
I got ready for work
Wearing pink and grey
And my winter coat
I was walking the dogs
There were tiny flurries of snow
Little flaky flecks of white
Fluttering near my face
My hand reached into my pocket
I put the phone to my ear

I was standing at the corner
– A crossroads –
When the day became anything but ordinary.

RECORD, REMEMBER, REFLECT

Think of a time when a grandparent made an ordinary day extraordinary, or when an ordinary day changed forever because of a grandparent's illness or passing.

_____

_____

_____

_____

_____

_____

_____

_____

_____

_____

_____

_____

_____

_____

_____

PROXIMITY

"the quality or state of being proximate, next, or very near (as in time, place, relationship) : immediate or close propinquity"

Once, Grandpa Peder and Grandma Alice came to help me in the form of a couple who sat next to me on an airplane.

I was flying home from California after a family visit. For weeks before the trip and especially while there, I was on the verge of breakdown and really had no business traveling or being around other people – especially loved ones.

After eleven months of life with triple negative breast cancer, my body was coming in for a dramatic landing, jostling and crashing and taxiing down the runway with the force of what those 333 odd days had brought me through.

I knew I wasn't happy. I knew I didn't feel like myself – far from my baseline of energetic, enthusiastic, and empathetic. But just how far off baseline, as in, living for weeks in a foreign country I'd never been to, yet still thinking I was in my homeland?

That was me.

I was in new territory. I had no map out of that place. I hadn't even packed a bag because I didn't know what I'd need there.

Depression is a strange thing.

Post-cancer depression, paired with premature menopause and post-traumatic stress disorder from cancer treatment, is also strange.

Cancer changes your body. Chemotherapy infusions change your body. Losing parts of your body in an hours-long surgery changes your body. Twenty-eight rounds of radiation changes your body.

Is there depression in my family? Yes. Like many other families, there's a history of depression and anxiety in mine. Family members on both sides, distant and present, who struggle with the dynamic duo.

I was still convinced I needed to get over some kind of hump, that I could get back on a schedule that didn't involve cancer, that I could get back into a routine like the one I was on before cancer so rudely and abruptly pushed me off course.

But when I was back in the place I thought I'd find myself again, I didn't.

As summer transitioned to fall, I didn't find my stride or cadence; I didn't find my gumption, grit, or anything I recognized.

I was finally alone again, a place I normally loved to be, and I hated it. But I didn't want anyone to come over.

I felt like I was stuck in my skin and simultaneously trying to crawl out of it.

I was pacing the floor but going nowhere, scaling the walls unsure of what was at the top, my brain splintering in directions it had never taken.

This was a level of depression that had been brewing for months but I didn't see it for what it was. This was a level of depression that found me apathetic and numb – despite a few months earlier feeling like I'd do whatever it took to get out of cancer alive.

How could I go from the person who was ruggedly resolved – despite chemo sapping every last cell of its life-giving strength – to the person who now entertained thoughts of falling with not a single worry of how she'd stick the landing?

That plane ride home changed everything. Not right away – but it was the tipping point.

I have a picture on my phone of the woman I sat next to (she knew people in Norway and in the US who are connected to my grandparents), but I'm not sure she was real. It still feels like a dream where my grandparents came to sit with me, to make sure I got home safely – from California, and from cancer.

I can't explain it any other way. But the more I've lived and learned – especially from the cancer world – the more I understand what people mean when they say the veil is thin. And I'm glad it was Grandma Alice and Grandpa Peder who pushed back the curtain that day.

This poem describes the many postures one may take when faced with a near-death experience.

Near Death

> If you ever have to look death straight in the eye,
> What will you see?
>
> What will you do?
>
> What will you learn?
>
> There's never been an easier next step.
> There's never been a harder next step.
>
> When you have a near-death experience,
> Or when you are forced to be near death –
> near to a person who has died –
>
> You might look away
> You might cower, shiver, crumble
>
> You might arch your back in resolve
> You might lower your head in resignation
> You might lift your eyes in wonder

None of these embodied responses are wrong.
All of these embodied responses are yours.

When I looked death straight in the eye,
I saw me.

RECORD, REMEMBER, REFLECT

Think of a time you felt close to your grandparents in an other-worldly way, or a time they came to you in a dream.

QUINTESSENCE

"the most perfect or rarest distillation or extract: the most typical example or representative : the consummate instance (as of a quality or class)"

How do you measure a person, especially one who was larger than life?

How do you find the right words to honor someone after they're gone, or describe them to people who never knew them?

Can you distill a person down to just one word?

Humans are complex creatures, and we encapsulate endless details. But we are also capable of stunning simplicity.

I believe that each person has a certain unique spirit about them that can be crystallized, like an atom, compacted and compounded into one glorious word.

And so, if I could only use one word to describe Grandma Donna, I'd choose: exuberance, which means "joyously unrestrained and enthusiastic."

If I could only use one word to describe Grandpa Peder, I'd choose: wholehearted, which means "undivided in purpose, enthusiasm, or will."

If I could only use one word to describe Grandma Alice, I'd choose: quietude,⁵ which means "a state of stillness, calmness, and quiet in a person or place."

And if I could only use one word to describe all three of the grandparents I had the joy of knowing well, I'd choose: precious, which means "of such extreme value that a suitable price is hard to estimate."

There is power in many words, and there's power in one.

This poem is the continuation of themes I discovered when writing the portrait of Great Grandma Agnes – one of resilience and also the sea.

Quintessence

How do you bottle up the sum and substance of a person,
And all their moving and messy and magnificent parts?

They're always changing,
Even when they're gone.
They're never really gone,
And that's why they're always changing.

So tell their stories,
In the now and then
Again and again and again ...
A message in a bottle
Washing up on the shores
A world contained within.

RECORD, REMEMBER, REFLECT

Choose one word that describes the essence of each of your grandparents.

REMINISCE

"to think, talk, or write about the past"

Reminiscing has always been a favorite pastime of mine, and I have no intentions of stopping. Little makes me happier than a walk down memory lane, especially if grandparent stories are involved.

And in such a digital-heavy culture as ours is today, I believe there's no better time to bring it back. We love vintage, we love nostalgia: why not make reminiscing a thing we love? A way of calling back the past that's not defeatist or depressing, and not a tactic for avoidance or denial. A way that embodies memories of what and who made us – without shame or blame.

To reminisce with someone – or just in the company of your own thoughts – requires slowing down: something we don't do enough of in our tap, swipe, thumb-through world.

Aren't so many of the things we love most on our screens related to reminiscing, remembering, and reliving the past? Vacation photos of memorable meals and picturesque views, TV commercials from decades ago, first day of school snapshots of our children over the years?

I'm in favor of bringing back the past: Not to stay there, but to absorb the delights our sweetest memories hold.

This poem contains some of my most cherished rememberings.

Rememberings

Remember, remember, remember...

Remember when Grandpa wrapped us up like burritos
And the blue pool towels were our soft tortillas?
Our shivering bodies at once calmed by the tightness
And the sunshine warming us
And Grandpa's happy smile.

Remember, remember, remember...

Remember when Grandma served us Silver Mints in the gazebo
And it was probably the first time we'd eaten in hours
because there was just too much swimming to do?
Cool mint ice cream in a thin tempered chocolate shell
that cracked when we bit into it,
Green ice cream dribbling down our chins and necks,
Mixing with the pool water,
And our laughter
And Grandma's happy smile.

Remember, remember, remember...

Remember when Grandma sang *"it's the most won-duh-full time,
of the yeee-uh"*
And made up her own words to Rudolph – *"Olive, the othuh
reindee-uh"* –
With a broad and cheeky grin
And a jolly lift in her voice?
It wasn't Christmas until then,
And I can't hear those jingles now without thinking of her
And her effervescent smile.

RECORD, REMEMBER, REFLECT

What's your favorite way to reminisce? By having conversations, looking at photos, visiting places that hold special significance, honoring traditions, or all of the above?

_____

_____

_____

_____

_____

_____

_____

_____

_____

_____

_____

_____

_____

_____

_____

STEEP

*"to saturate with or subject thoroughly to (some strong or
pervading influence)"*

As I sit here typing these words, a new cup of tea steeps, the steam
rises, the leaves of peppermint and spearmint soaking alongside rose
hips, lemon peel, and hibiscus, infusing the hot water with depth and
life, flavor and richness.

We are steeped in our stories.

I believe that who we are and who we will be is steeped in the memories of our ancestors, steeped in the genes of our tribes – of birth and
of choosing – infused by things we can't forget, things we didn't know
to remember, and bits of fact and fancy in between.

I believe there are stories we may only know in our bodies, stories
which may never be told to another living being on a book's pages or
in a person's retelling around a table or a campfire. But our lived stories are just as real, and just as much a part of us as our eye color and
hair texture. We owe it to ourselves to listen once in a while.

I believe that, like those concrete, compact ingredients gathered in
the square microcosm of a tea bag, which – when paired with heat –
transform the most basic of elements into something so soothing and
magical and real, the concrete, compact facts of our life bleeds into
our lived stories. And with each retelling or discovery, with each new

experience, we steep and steep and steep a history that's impossible to pin down but as essential to life as water.

Grandpa Peder loved sugar cubes. I don't know if it was their concentrated sweetness, coarse texture, or their precise shape. Maybe it was the way they tasted when soaked in dark strong coffee. But I never knew anyone who loved sugar cubes like Grandpa, and his delight in them – and mine in sitting beside him while he drank his coffee and ate the coffee-soaked crystals – is perhaps what I'm recreating when I sprinkle raw sugar on my morning chai. Little tiny potent pieces that crunch under my tongue as I sip, remembering, remembering, remembering...

My memories of Grandpa Peder in his workshop are steeped in sawdust.

To this day, the scent and sight of sawdust instantly transports me there: a little girl covering her ears at the sound of the saw, her curls pushing out through her fingers. Watching the wood sparks fly up and drop to the floor in a neat, soft, aromatic pile. Watching his steady hands guide the wood through the tablesaw like it was a piece of precious fabric. Watching his work-worn hands wipe the fine dust away, leaving behind wood as smooth as silk.

I loved touching it then, when I could lift my hands off my ears and come stand next to him, me in my shorts and flip flops and he in his denim striped overalls and boots, the pair of us surrounded by the sawdust puddles and the fragrance of freshly cut wood.

It fascinated me, the way a coarse square of sandpaper – as grainy and gritty as a sugar cube – could soften a rough piece of wood to the fluid silkiness of paper, leaving behind shavings as soft and splintery as my curls.

That tiny little square dissolved the shards of pine or walnut or cherry, melting them away like the sugar cube in Grandpa Peder's coffee, refining and transforming the surface through the heated friction from the hands above it, satisfying like a steeped cup of tea and a story you feel in the warmth of your hands wrapped around it.

This poem was based on using the word steep in a totally different way than in the stories above, and I was pleasantly surprised by where it led me.

Steep

The fjord walls are steep
like grandma and grandpa's driveway
and the path to grandma's *hytte**
winding up the hill in Herad
with the green, green farmland below
where the white and brown horses
are lining the fence
reflecting the tones of the *kirke***
and the dark moss-covered stones of my great grandparents
nestled between the mustard colored farmhouse
with the wooden screen door
overlooking the road below
at the edge of the earth
and the road to my house
climbing up the mountain
leading to my home away from their homeland
a place where they reside
in the cardinals that visit the feeders
and the rocks we stand on
to look out at the twinkling lights
of the valley below

My heart is here
And my heart is there
And my heart is home here.
And my heart is home there too.

*cottage in Norwegian, or *sommerhus* (summer house), used by the family for getaways
  throughout the year

**church in Norwegian

RECORD, REMEMBER, REFLECT

What traditions steeped in story are part of your family's heritage?

_____

_____

_____

_____

_____

_____

_____

_____

_____

_____

_____

_____

_____

_____

_____

_____

_____

TENDER

"gentleness and affection"

When the sun went down, so did Grandpa Peder and Grandma Alice.

After dinner, they'd plant themselves on a couch in a small sitting room – surrounded by books and pictures of their family – for an evening in front of the tube.

To the left of the couch was a telephone and a window, the essentials of grandparents whose family lived down the street. Any passing car was prey to their vision.

In between the couch and the television was a small table, strewn with bills and numerous letters from Ed McMahon, notifying Mr. Peder Pedersen that he indeed may be the grand-prize winner! *The Nordisk Tidene* (*Norway Times*) and a *Bibelen* (Bible) lay among the scattering of junk mail.

On this particular night when I came to visit, Judge Judy was on, and the room was dark, lit only by the glare of the television. I plopped down on the couch right in between them, wedged in *koselig* (cozy) style.

Grandpa was relaxed in his favorite navy blue cardigan sweater and plaid shirt, slippers, and slacks (a word that will forever make me think of him anytime I hear it). Grandma was in a soft pink cotton button-down shirt, slacks, and slippers, and she always sat quietly, reserved in manner and body, by her window post.

As they watched the show, Grandpa would throw his head back, slap his thigh, and laugh so loudly he was practically snorting. "Can you believe these idiots?" he said, turning to me, his eyes shining with tears.

Every so often, headlights broke the darkness outside the window, and they'd snap to attention.

"Who was that?" asked Grandpa, leaning forward and straining eyes and neck to identify the car. Grandma Alice pushed the curtains back ever so slightly, peeking through the sheer fabric. "I [tink] it was Steve," she answered, still looking out the window. Satisfied with the answer, they both leaned back to resume watching the show.

My grandparents' curiosity might be misconstrued as nosiness, but I knew it was more than that. It was their way of caring for the people they loved most. But their sometimes-overbearing concern was ironic: because a year after their marriage in 1949, they left all family ties in Norway, came to America, and never moved back to their homeland.

"So that's why you moved the TV into this room, right? So you can see who drives by at night?" I teased.

"Oh no, it's not me that worries," Grandma said defensively as she cocked her head towards Grandpa. "It's Pop," she whispered, grinning as she pointed at him.

"Are you [yokin']?" said Grandpa, looking at her directly with more admiration than frustration. "You're the one [dat's] always sittin' by [de] window." I leaned back in my chair, laughing to myself as they bickered for a few minutes over who worried the most.

These moments were some of my favorites, squished in between them on the couch, soaking it all in. I treasure those tender, uneventful, and mostly quiet evenings – with the exception of their precious squabbles with one another.

Many times I was restless while sitting there, but I'm grateful for the times I slowed down enough to "sit and stay awhile." And now, whenever I sit at my writing desk by the window, I often find myself looking out to see if anyone's coming down the driveway – and I smile at this potentially genetic behavior.

This poem was inspired by the way my grandparents talked to each other, which was really more like arguing but in the most benign and adorable way.

What does a lifelong love look like?

Theirs was a love that was tender
even in the bickering
that seemed constant
in my younger mind

and now that I've been married as many years
as I was when I watched them love in their own way

I understand their love
and the way they loved
even in the bickering
and in all the things I didn't hear them say

except

in the bickering,
there was so much love
in between the words.

RECORD, REMEMBER, REFLECT

Think of a tender moment(s) with your grandparents. Recall the details, the feelings, the surroundings. Reinvent the scene.

_____

_____

_____

_____

_____

_____

_____

_____

_____

_____

_____

_____

_____

_____

_____

_____

_____

_____

_____

UPEYGAN

"black rhinoceros"

"Evuh since upeygan school, ya think ya so smaht."
– Grandma Donna

For as long as I live, this will be the definition of upeygan. A strange word that actually means black rhinoceros, but is indelibly etched in my memory in the musical diction of Grandma Donna's Brooklyn-Italian accent and don't mess attitude.

Grandma Donna was the life of the party but never the center of attention. I don't know how she managed it but it came as naturally to her as breathing.

It was a lazy weekend afternoon and we were all gathered in my aunt's window-lined family room playing a game of Balderdash.

As a side note: everyone played board games in our family, from the youngest grandkids who barely understood the concept or directions all the way up to Grandma. And for some reason – not because she wasn't smart or because we thought her foolish – we were always surprised by how well she'd play the game du jour.

Maybe it's because she didn't seem to be around when the game was being explained. Somehow, she was able to listen and fully absorb the rules of play without looking in the direction of the speaker or even being in the same room.

And so, after the speaker read out loud the unusual-but-actual word on the Balderdash game card, a designated person would gather everyone's made-up definitions once they'd had some time to think and write. Then, the reading would begin.

"Evuh since upeygan school, ya think ya so smaht."

I don't remember who read Grandma's answer out loud that day. But it doesn't really matter, because it couldn't be read in any other way than in her distinctive tone of voice, the way I hear it in my brain even today, decades later.

"Evuh since upeygan school, ya think ya so smaht."

We roared with laughter at her wit.

We roared with laughter at her command of language.

We roared with laughter because no one could say things like Grandma could.

And when I piped up with – *"Grandma, you're not supposed to write it so we know it's yours!"* – we roared with laughter again, because at that point, as Grandma would say, *"Who cayuz?"* (cares, in Brooklyn-Italian), and technically, she was the champion of the game for all time with a definition like that.

Speaking of the champion for all time, in the kitchen and on the dinner table, Grandma's flavors were always as winningly bold as the way she spoke.

The sausages she made with the unmistakable earthiness of fennel were always paired with mildly seasoned meatballs that were only mildly seasoned so they could complement the bright and zesty forthrightness of the sauce.

To this day, her Italian food wins every time for me. I've had authentic, handmade, artisan Italian food that's out-of-this-world delicious. I've had Italian food at restaurants and at people's houses that I'd eat again and again.

But nothing I've ever had – even things made by Italian relatives – ever comes close to tasting like Grandma's homemade sausage, meatballs, or sauce.

Even the way she prepared pasta – the noodles that had just the right amount of crunch without being raw – had her imprint, an unmatched taste, the fingerprint of her forefathers and mothers who rolled pasta dough and stirred sauces and mixed meats and spices on tiled-and-clay hearths in Calabria or over bonfires on the beaches of the Italian coast.

There was so much palpable joy in her cooking. But perhaps the most remarkable joy of all was the way she'd join her family at the table to savor her culinary handiwork with them.

Some cooks spend so much time bustling in the background, zealously bringing plates and pots and endlessly passing around piles of food – but never actually sitting down long enough to eat them.

Not Grandma.

She knew how to cook, she knew how to serve, and she knew how to sit down and eat with exuberant abandon, elevating pasta, sauce, sausage, and meatballs to the level of kings and queens, making every meal and mouthful a mirthful celebration.

This is the place I miss her the most.

This is the place I yearn for every time my sisters and I go to the San Gennaro Festival in New York City. This is the whisper I hear when my neighbor invites us for "Sunday sauce," and he makes pasta by hand and hangs it to dry over his butcher block countertop while the spices, oil, veggies, and tomatoes simmer on the stove.

There will never be a recipe that brings her vibrant sauce back to life, replicates her textures, or embodies her fennel-laced sausage. But at every boisterous gathering around a board of heart-made foods I attend, I will relish every bite with the same gusto as if she were sitting at the head of the table – as she always did – with her big smile, her bigger laugh, and her ever-moving, story-telling hands.

This poem refers to Grandma Donna's endearing practice of defacing certain old photographs.

Upeygan

In my mind the black rhinoceros
Is the color of the marker
She'd use to color over
Faces she didn't want to see anymore

RECORD, REMEMBER, REFLECT

What's a funny saying or phrase that your grandparent(s) frequently used?

VOCATION

"the work in which a person is regularly employed usually for pay : line of work : occupation"

Grandpa Peder had a traditional mindset when it came to women working, but as the son of a working midwife, there was some wiggle room. And good thing, because he had eight granddaughters!

Although he seemed to prefer a woman staying busy with the work of the home, he was not opposed to any of the career aspirations his girls would float past him. He always supported my dreams of being a writer. He never shot down the idea or said things like "You'll never make any money that way."

All of my grandparents worked hard: in their jobs, in their retirement roles, and in grandparenting most of all. That was the vocation they were meant for, in my opinion. That was the job they did best – and probably because it was the one they cherished most.

This poem offers a glimpse into my grandparents' jobs and the ways they connect to my own.

Vocation

My grandpa built houses with wood and his hands,
and I build houses with words and my hands.

Pencil shavings, sawdust shavings,
Sketches of stories, blueprints for building,
Pencils used in both of our crafts.

Aircrafts inspected and cleared for ascent
At the behest of his hands.
I imagine the grandpa I didn't meet in this life
Always had a pencil tucked behind his ear.

The clackety-clack of the keys on a typewriter
In her first job after girl's school
The rubbery hum of the soles of her shoes
Walking to work in New York City
My grandmothers worked with their feet and their hands

And the tradition of hard work goes on.

RECORD, REMEMBER, REFLECT

What were/are your grandparents' jobs? Have you followed in their foot-steps in any way, or do you plan to in a future career?

WORN

"to impair or diminish by use or attrition : consume or waste gradually"

Each one of my grandparents had such a distinct sense of style – and it matched their personalities perfectly. They all knew how to dress up and look sharp for a special occasion, but they also knew how to be comfortable and utilitarian in their day-to-day activities.

When I think of Grandpa Peder, I think of his favorite Izod cardigans paired with a flannel shirt, dungarees (what he called jeans), and soft slippers when the day was done.

When I think of Grandma Alice, I think of her in crisply pressed cotton button-down tops, in light pink or purple, with white slacks and leather clogs. I never saw her in a pair of jeans.

When I think of Grandma Donna, I think of her beaming face in a picture, and she's wearing a red button-down dress with white polka dots and white slip-on shoes. Her smile is so big, it practically jumps out of the photo.

I am grateful to have one of Grandpa Peder's *lusekoftes* (a heavy wool Norwegian sweater). It's blue and white with pewter clasps and a reindeer design, and I wear it when I want to feel close to him. I wore it often while writing this book.

Clothing may not last – unless it's a *lusekofte*, built for decades of wear in frigid temperatures – but pictures in our minds and photo albums do. But probably the most memorable thing all of my grandparents wore was their joy in grandparenting. And what a gift it was to be a recipient of their adornment.

This poem is inspired by my stylish maternal grandparents and the leather jackets they wore to church.

sunday mornings in winter

> A soft leather jacket reminds me
> Of Sunday mornings in winter,
> Standing next to them,
> Singing hymns,
> Their black leather jackets laying behind us on the pew,
> The old rugged cross he made with his hands
> Hanging at the front of the building
> He built with his hands
> And her hands, soft and worn, squeezing mine,
> That filled many punch bowls in the church basement kitchen
> And carried many platters of waffles, butter, and jam
> To fellowship hall dinners.

RECORD, REMEMBER, REFLECT

Do you have a favorite piece of clothing that was your grandparents? What do you picture them wearing when you think of them in the past?

XYLEM

"a complex tissue in the vascular system of higher plants consisting of vessels, tracheids, or both usually together with wood fibers and parenchyma cells, functioning chiefly in conduction but also in support and storage, and typically constituting the woody element (as of a plant stem)"

It's rather ironic that his two sons rarely board a plane without fear and trembling, but at the peak of his career as a lead inspector for Lockheed Aircraft, no plane ever left the ground without Grandpa Warren's approval.

Grandpa Warren serviced military and commercial planes alike, and eventually received clearance to work on presidential aircraft, having first been vetted by the Secret Service, who came to question neighbors and friends.

I imagine him as a young boy in his room, piecing together the delicate parts of a model airplane, enjoying every satisfying connection of notched Balsa sliding into place with a soft click. I wonder if he heard the sounds of a roaring jet engine in his future life as a presidential aircraft inspector bottled up in that micro moment...

His mom, Great Grandma Agnes, calls him down for dinner, and it's only then he realizes he's spent the entire day in his room working on the model. He appreciates that she didn't stop him for lunch, and at this point, he's finished his 26th model plane of the summer – so he might as well have dinner before he starts the 27th...

Actual airplane wings are constructed of aerospace grade aluminum mixed with a metal that harnesses the strength of steel. But it's the support system hidden within the wings that gives a plane its launching power and lift, an intricate, intentional, complicated, and comprehensive webbing below the smooth aerodynamic surface that cuts through clouds and atmospheric pressure.[6]

It strikes me that such common materials as wood and metal, known for being solid in substance and structurally sound, can also be incredibly thin and strategically lightweight, enough to lift a plane off the ground.

But then, it's all about the support system, isn't it? And if you ask me, grandparents – honorary or given – are the roots and the wings.

This poem is about your roots, literally and figuratively.

Xylem

Who is in your root system?
Who brings the water up and down the wooden stem
That runs from your head to your sternum
Then trickles to your toes and soles
That are rooted to the ground?

What makes you feel "rooted?" Are/were your grandparents part of your support system, hidden or otherwise?

YEARNING

CHAPTER 25

*"the act of one that yearns : eager or anxious longing :
tender compassion"*

There's a word from Welsh culture – *hiraeth* – and it means a "deep longing for something, especially one's home."[7]

It's a blend of "homesickness, nostalgia, and longing," a "pull on the heart," and a feeling that "conveys a distinct feeling of missing something irretrievably lost."[8]

This is what I feel every day as I walk through life without my grandparents. This is what I feel every time I see a picture of Norway, or see a grandfather holding his granddaughter, or hear a song that makes me think of my Italian ancestors.

What if we never really lose anything though?

What if the things we think are irretrievably lost are just hidden from view because we are looking in the wrong direction, or with eyes fixed on certainty rather than mystery?

What if we let the longing pull our hearts towards seeing unknowns as imagined possibilities, if we replaced longing and missing and homesickness with abundance and declaration and a history we can hang our hats on, a welcome mat we can walk across, a home of memories we can live in, with the decor being both real and "perhapsed" into place?

What if the thin veil was like the sheer curtains in Grandma Alice and Grandpa Peder's sitting room, and on the other side were all the people we wanted to see, and we could sit and stay awhile and chat with them, all *koselig* (cozy) on the couch, with bottomless pots of coffee and tea?

What if the thin veil was like the flower petals in the little girl's flying braids at the Maypole celebration on the Italian mountain top, and Great Grandpa Anthony just kept pouring bottles of wine, and all the guests at the party kept twirling pasta around their forks and never got to the bottom of the plate?

We can live in the land of imagination. We can be at home in our imaginings. What we imagine is true if it's our own, and even if it's paired with a reality that's past or present, that doesn't make it any less true. Your imagination is your own property, your garden to tend, your house and home and heart and head.

What a comfort writing this book has been to me, even as I longed for the characters of these stories to jump out of the pages and give me a good strong standing hug or hearty pats on the back. Or to pass me a wool blanket I could make into a cape to shield me from any other earthly tragedies or trials I may still endure.

Will I meet my beloveds and their beloveds in another world someday? I hope so.

Will that other world be vibrant with color and story and echoes and reminiscences? I hope so.

Will that other world show us which stories were lasting – everlasting – because they were real, and will the gaps I've filled in with "perhaps" be transformed by a single thread running through one giant piece of tapestry?

Maybe. But, does it matter?

At this point, I believe what matters more is not whether the stories I imagined or heard or "perhapsed" into being are true. The people in them were real, were mine, are part of me, are part of history and the future.

And it's the people behind the stories that matter most. While the details are important, they're not the whole story. The genes that make up our flesh and blood, quirks and tendencies, hair texture and diseases are indestructible bits of living matter passed from one generation to the next to infinity. They're tied to our lived stories, which are inevitably full of knowns and unknowns. And to keep those stories alive, we must keep discovering them – and passing them on.

How they're remembered changes from generation to generation, but in each retelling, those people and their stories live again, and live anew. They're alive on the tip of your tongue at a family gathering story circle, or on the page of a descendant's high school history report.

Let your stories live, and keep your loved ones alive, always.

This poem is inspired by my lifelong obsession with grandparents.

My First Loves

Every time I pick up a new grandparent,
I yearn for mine all the more.
(I know you can't just buy a replacement grandparent
like a new set of dishes from the store)

But still I try to fill that void.

And love in the form
of an honorary grandparent
can fill the place that's empty –

But not entirely.

Because my heart
forever belongs
to my first loves,
my beloved
grandparents.

RECORD, REMEMBER, REFLECT

When you feel homesick for your grandparents, what anchors you?

ZEST

"a quality of enhancing enjoyment : piquancy : keen enjoyment : relish, gusto"

I'd never want to live in a world where there are no grandparents. My daughter currently has all four grandparents in her life, and I'm so grateful for that. She still picks up "extraordinary" grandparents (her translation of the word "honorary") all the time.

I've taught her well.

Life without grandparents is like a sauce without spices, or like a hug without hands. It's just not the same, and they're the most important part.

The recipe for a life well-lived is one that's steeped in reminiscing and imagining, one that's rooted in ancestors and love and descendants and legacy.

I may not be as adept in the kitchen as my grandmothers were. I certainly do not have the mechanical proficiency of my grandfathers. But what they all taught me is to live with relish and gusto, to practice modesty sparingly when it comes to big feelings or stories, and to pass around heaps and heaps and heaps of love.

This poem is inspired by the language of my Italian ancestors, and the way they loved life.

the spice of life is actually zest

Scorza is zest in Italian,
And its cousins are:
: *il gusto* :
: *il entusiasmo* :
: *il aroma* :

With siblings like:
Taste and relish,
Enthusiasm and flavor,
Fragrance and spice.

And I couldn't think of better
letters combined to make
my Italian ancestors come to life.

What brings your grandparents to life?

Grandma

I want to be the kind of person
who is fun to grow old with
with pearl white hair
set in curlers everyday
grandchildren surrounding me
as my laugh-lined eyes
read stories that I've written.

written in a journal on December 29, 1998

ENDNOTES

1. Revelation 1:19, *The Holy Bible, Modern English Version.* Military Bible Association, Charisma House, 2014.

2. Ray Bradbury, *Now and Forever: Somewhere a Band Is Playing & Leviathan.* Harper, 2008, 2007.

3. *Merriam-Webster's Unabridged Dictionary*, Merriam-Webster, https://unabridged.merriam-webster.com/. Accessed 17 Feb. 2023

4. Lisa Knopp, "Perhapsing": The Use of Speculation in Creative Nonfiction. Brevity, https://brevitymag.com/craft-essays/perhapsing-the-use-of-speculation-in-creative-nonfiction/. Accessed 17 Feb. 2023.

5. "Quietude," Oxford Languages Dictionary, OED Online. Oxford University Press, Accessed 17 Feb. 2023.

6. Tony Bingelis, "Wood Wings," Experimental Aircraft Association (EAA). https://www.eaa.org/eaa/aircraft-building/builderresources/while-youre-building/building-articles/wood/wood-wings , Accessed 17 Feb. 2023.

7. Cailey Rizzo, "Why Your Airplane's Wings Will Never Snap Off," Travel + Leisure. https://www.travelandleisure.com/travel-news/can-airplane-wings-snap-off. Accessed 17 Feb. 2023.

8   Lily Crossley-Baxter, "The untranslatable word that connects Wales," BBC Travel. https://www.bbc.com/travel/article/20210214-the-welsh-word-you-cant-translate. Accessed 17 Feb. 2023.

ACKNOWLEDGMENTS

There are hundreds of people who have helped me become a published author, and their names could fill a book.

My most faithful and long standing cheerleaders include my loving parents, Bill & Linda, who have generously and consistently nurtured my love of writing since day one – in seen and unseen ways.

I am deeply grateful to my husband Joshua and daughter Naya for their patience with me when I'm in writing mode. And for the excitement shared and encouragement given by my four sisters, Kerri, Debbie, Laurie, and Nadine; my 9 precious nieces and nephews; and my family-in-law by love and marriage, "Grammy" Jean, "Poppa" Jim, Wade, Derek, Wade, Jared, and Dezerai, I'm so very blessed.

Gratitude also goes to the family members who provided further insights into my grandparents' lives.

For the generous gifts of childcare so I could complete this book on time, I am grateful to my family and to the honorary grandparents in our lives: Nina & Mike and Debbie & Scott.

For the generous gift of a quiet cottage where I could write for hours without interruption and in beautiful surroundings, I am grateful to Carol & Paul.

For the gift of encouraging texts, cards, calls, conversations, life-enriching and sustaining friendship, and many other forms of support, I am grateful to Alicia, Amy, Christa, Megan, Kristen, Bonnie, Laura, Joanne, Rosanne, Amy, Teresa, and countless others.

I also want to express gratitude to my college English professors who've become friends and lifelong mentors, my writing colleagues and "writer friends" I've met through various writing jobs and online writer communities, and my readers – the people near and far who've followed my work since I started putting pen to paper.

It takes a village to write a book; thanks for being part of mine.

ABOUT THE AUTHOR

Michelle Seitzer has been writing since she was old enough to hold a pen. Her brain is constantly running in writer mode, capturing daily details, formulating chapter titles, and archiving memories to be made into stories. Her first love has always been words. A caregiver, entrepreneur, and breast cancer survivor, Michelle lives in Pennsylvania with her family, and loves to collect books and honorary grandparents. Find out more at michelleseitzer.com.

Made in the USA
Monee, IL
18 April 2023

32068868R00080